*Robin Robertson*

# HILL OF DOORS

PICADOR

First published 2013 by Picador
an imprint of Pan Macmillan, a division of Macmillan Publishers Limited
Pan Macmillan, 20 New Wharf Road, London N1 9RR
Basingstoke and Oxford
Associated companies throughout the world
www.panmacmillan.com

ISBN 978-1-4472-3153-0 HB
ISBN 978-1-4472-3154-7 PB

A CIP catalogue record for this book is available from the British Library.

Printed and bound by CPI Group (UK) Ltd, Croydon, CR0 4YY

Visit www.picador.com to read more about all our books
and to buy them. You will also find features, author interviews and
news of any author events, and you can sign up for e-newsletters
so that you're always first to hear about our new releases.

*for Karin*

*let us not forget that the greatest man*
*is never more than an animal*
*disguised as a god*

Picabia

# Contents

HILL OF DOORS

# ANNUNCIATION

*after Fra Angelico*

He has come from the garden, leaving
no shadow, no footprint in the dew.
They hold each other's gaze at the point
of balance: everything streaming
towards this moment, streaming away.

A word will set the seed
of life and death,
the over-shadowing of this girl
by a feathered dark.
But not yet: not quite yet.

How will she remember the silence
of that endless moment?
Or the end, when it all began –
the first of seven joys
before the seven sorrows?

She will remember the aftersong
because she is only human.
One day
she'll wake with wings, or wake
and find them gone.

# THE COMING GOD

*after Nonnus*

Horned child, double-born into risk, guarded
by satyrs, centaurs, raised
by the nymphs of Nysa, by the Hyades:
here he was, the toddler, Dionysus.
He cried 'Daddy!' stretching up to the sky, and he was right
and clever, because the sky *was* Zeus
his father, reaching down.

As he grew, he learnt to flit through other forms;
he'd become a newborn kid, shivering in the corner,
his soft pink skin suddenly the pelt of a goat
and the goat bleating, his hands and feet
now taking their first steps on tottering hooves.

As a grown boy, he would show himself
as a girl, in saffron robes and veils,
moulding his hips
to the coil of a woman's body,
shaping his lips to speak in a woman's voice.

At nine he started to hunt.
He could match the jink
of a coursing hare, reach down at speed
and trip it over; chase alongside a young buck and just
lift it from the running ground
and swing it over his shoulder.

He tamed the wild beasts, just by talking,
and they knelt to be petted, harnessed in.
By his boyhood's end he was dressing in their skins:
the tiger's tree-line stripe, the fallow deer speckled
like a fall of stars,
the pricked ears of the lynx.

One day he came upon a maddened she-bear
and reached out his right hand to her snout
and put his white fingers to her mouth, her teeth,
his fingers gentle at the bristled jaw,
which slackened
and drew in a huge breath
covering the hand of Dionysus with kisses,
wet, coarse, heavy kisses.

## A CHILDHOOD

The last bottle of lemonade is nodding
in the rock pool, keeping cold. A childhood,
put away for later. I'm too busy to notice
the sun is going, that they're packing up,
that it's almost time for home. The low waves
warm round my knees as I dig in,
panning for light, happy to be here, dreaming
of the evening I'll wake on the lilo
singing my head off, somewhere
in the sea-lanes to Stavanger, or Oslo.

## 1964

Under the gritted lid of winter
each ice-puddle's broken plate
cracked to a star. The morning
assembling itself into black and white, the slow dawn
its developing tray. Cold steams off the grass;
the frosted yarrow and sea holly
smoke in the new sun.

\*

In the barber-shop mirror, I study this museum of men
through glass: their shaving brushes, talc and whetted razors,
the bottles of bay rum, hair tonic, astringents; long
leather strops; those faded photographs of hairstyles,
that blue Barbicide jar on the counter
dense with pickled combs and scissors like a failed aquarium;
the special drawer full of Durex, copies of *Parade*.

\*

The plane from England scores a skater's track
across the icy sky; on the promenade, frost
thistles the railings. You hear the drawl
of the wave, the gulls, raucous at their bins,
the day's first Labrador, his tail flogging the surf.
The quarantined city lies behind, bilge-deep in cobbles,
listing: flying the Yellow Jack, typhoid in its quick-work.

On the floor of the butcher's,
blood has rolled through the sawdust
and become round and soft.
We found the blood-buds
in corners as the shop was closing, and gathered
the biggest ones in handkerchiefs to take them
to the woods, break them open for their jelly.

*

In the light from the blaze, there's a fox
nailed to a fence-post: the tricked god
hanging from his wounds. We have nothing to feed
to the fire's many beaks but some mealy apples
and a bottle of Hay's Lemonade, which explodes.
I dig in my pockets and find
a Salvation Army picture of Jesus; tender it to the flame.

*

We'd skip school lunches for some milk,
a rowie and a mutton pie. A twist
of penny sweets: foam bananas, liquorice sticks.
On special days, some hard bonfire toffee
and a lucky bag, watching the third-years fight
in the kirkyard, in among the graves. One boy
holds the other's hair so he can kick him in the face.

\*

Creels are swung from boat to shore, filling
fishboxes in silver rows. A slush of ice and gulls
all day till nightfall. Then all you hear is the ice
tightening back together
and the cats crying that dreadful way they have,
like the sound of babies singing
lullabies to other babies.

\*

I knew how children came, so I look for the stork
in the cliffs over the mussel pools,
in the quarry ledges, the chimney stacks,
all along the walking pylons –
search for her everywhere
in the gantries of the storm woods, in the black pines,
that she might take me back.

# UNDER BEINN RUADHAINN

*for Andrew O'Hagan*

Three moons in the sky
the night they found him
drowned in Sawtan's Bog;
just his cap, sitting there
and his wee fat hands poking out.

It was no loss to the village,
I told them next morning,
and the villagers agreed.
Horn-daft, he was,
havering and glaikit
and scaring the children.

I mind that time
he picked up a mouse and ate it, quick,
in two mouthfuls;
set the tail aside
on the ground
like a cocktail stick.

I used her well, after that,
his Jennie,
still in her widow's weeds,
gilping into her
whenever I could,
in the barn or the boat-house
or off in the fields.
She slipped two or three out at least,
and sank each one in a lobster creel.

Her head was away
by the end, as mad as her man
and no good to me.
She sleeps now
under Beinn Ruadhainn, her face
covered in ivy,
scab, and sticky-willow.

Then the dreams came.
Last night: the burning loch,
so full of bairns
they bobbed to the surface
with their hair on fire;
black snow; rain
like razorblades;
the foosty-faced man,
there at every corner,
hands furred with grey-mould.
And her, as always,
star-naked, hatching
in the herring-nets.
The last I remember was my body
being driven with sticks through the town
to Sawtan's Brae, and hanged.

I broke from sleep and sat up in the dark.
I groped around for the matches
and the matches were put in my hand.

# CORRYVRECKAN

'a depe horlepoole quhairin if schippis do enter thair is no refuge
but death onlie'
Alexander Lindsay, *A Rutter of the Scottish Seas*, c. 1540


Thickening in these narrows to some height and speed,
squeezing through the Great Door, Dorus Mhor,
the sea's so high it's climbing over itself to get through.
They call these 'the overfalls'. A sluice through a bottleneck.
A great seething. The frenzy of water feeding on water.

Seen from above, the tidal race is a long army moving fast
across a plain as flat and grey as a shield of polished steel,
to reach, at the end, the terrible turbulence of battle.
A blue stream turned to a gutter of broken water:
water that's stood its ground, churning; sea
kept back and held in standing waves:
walls of water, each as tall as a church door,
endlessly breaking on the same point –
each wave swallowing its own form
and returning, re-making itself, chained there
on its own wheel, turning black to white to black.

The sea gets stranger beyond the sentry waves –
a round of slow slack-water, barely moving,
ringed by raging white: a close,
oily calm, unnaturally smooth, like a metal blank.
Then you see them – these
errors on the still surface – sudden
disturbances, boils that bulge and blister, burst,
small holes that appear, whirling open
as if a hundred sink-plugs had been pulled.

Then the huge round rises up: dead-level, streaming,
upwelling, holding its shape like some giant plate
that's been lying just under the water
being lifted up fast and then
dropped back down, the sea
sucking in after it,
from all sides, into its absence, waves
shearing over, folding in to the core, the depth
and the great black gullet of loss.
The maelstrom. The long throat of Corryvreckan.
The opened body of water that today we rode across.

# A QUICK DEATH

*'It is not.'*
Samuel Beckett

Blue-shelled, blue-blooded,
with eight legs, two
stalked eyes and a toothed stomach.
Heraldic: *azure, attired,*
*armed at all points, in pride.*

At rest, a blue-black gauntlet;
at war, a clacking samurai in lacquered plates, a fighter
swaying with his huge gloves, leading
with the smaller claw – the pincher, the seizer –
holding back the crusher, letting it drag.

The face, a tool-chest, a cutler's dream,
five sets of exterior mouthparts, a team of blades
moving constantly; the fantail skirt
splays open, the swimmerets
scissoring underneath.

\*

The three ante-rooms of death: the creel's
'kitchen' and 'parlour', and this restaurant tank
which we might as well call 'the larder'. The lobster
shuffles across its floor and taps the glass
twice, claws muffled by rubber bands.

The forecast is for stormy weather. Read it
in the glass, my fine dark handsome stranger;
it's the same for us all in the end –
a short journey: eyes first
into the fire.

# DIONYSUS IN LOVE

*after Nonnus*

Hardened by the hills of Phrygia,
quickened by its streams, the boy-god
Dionysus came of age.

And as his own body changed
his eyes grew wider, and turned
towards the bodies of others.
Ampelos was the one, above all:
most beautiful boy, most beautiful
of satyrs: lean and long and new.
Even his flaws were gorgeous:
the bony nubs at the forehead, that slight
skip in his step, sometimes;
the way he slept in a curve, his soft tail
slacked over his haunches.

Dionysus let him win at wrestling: flesh
on flesh, their knotted hands, legs
pressed against legs.
Then to feel those muscles of his
tighten in the flank
and flip him over,
so he could lie still under that weight.

Dionysus held back at the sprint,
to watch: the god
of spark and springheel, the god

who would cross continents with a single step
stood still, and with one breath
blew speed into his love's young body,
lifting it over the line.

Their race in the red river was the last test,
and glowing Ampelos matched it, red for red,
his colour rising as he met it,
rose to rose, and swept past Dionysus
who had watched him
from the corner of his eye,
and slowed.

The boy hoisted himself up from the river
streaming in victory, and went to the forest
where he gathered vipers to bind in his hair,
killed a deer for its dappled skin,
and leapt on the back of a mountain bear
and rode him out of the wood, all in imitation
of the god Dionysus.

Who stood, watching Ampelos.
Then drew him close, with a warning,
saying the boy need not fear
the sharp mouths of panthers, lions or bears,
only dread the horns of beasts –
for he had seen a horned dragon
rise from the rocks
with a fawn on its back
which it tossed down onto the stone altar,
gored it through

and feasted.
He had seen the blood fork
over the rocks into pools, pools
that filled and fell again
like some long dark drink
that spilled out thickly, slug
after slug, till it slowed
and dripped to a stop.

Dionysus watched him; never tired of watching,
though fearful now, for what he had seen.

And Ampelos watched him back,
every day, Dionysus
riding away on the saddle of a panther
to hunt the dark woods
with his maenads, with his deer-skin
whipping behind him,
out on the hunt
like a god.

And as he watched, he felt a presence
at his shoulder saying
'Why should *he* have the panthers,
why should *he* be the grand one?
Why don't you ride at his side
on the back of a bull, to please
the bull-king, for him to see you
with a bull between your knees?
The girl Europa
rode one bareback over our great sea

with no reins or bridle;
surely you can take a bull
and master it –
surely you can ride the forest?'
And as he turned
there was no one there.

And then the forest parted, and there it stood:
the bull, its huge mouth slopped open,
a grey tongue thick as the boy's arm
hung out in a curl
like some third horn
as it lowered its head to the running stream
and drank.
And as it drank, Ampelos pulled up rushes,
plaiting some into a bridle,
twisting others round an alder stem
to make a kind of whip.
Then he gathered lilies and anemones,
hyacinths and roses from the river bank
and strung them through, in a garland.
The bull stood, patiently,
and bent its head for the boy,
who stroked its brow, felt
the hard weight of its horns –
horns he dressed in flowers to the tips –
before he swung up on the bull's back,
slipped on the bridle, and called out
to Selene, goddess of the horned moon,
gleaming bull-driver in the night sky,
shouting 'Look! I am riding the horned bull!'

And the sky-goddess looked down
at this satyr, and sent him a reward
for his insolence: a gadfly –
goad and tormentor of beasts.
With the first sting the bull lurched forward
into a run, the second driving it wild
and away from the river up through the rocks,
maddened into a gallop, the boy
hanging on, the beast plunging higher
into the mountains,
trying to shake off the stinging fly.
In its frenzy the bull
bucked so hard
it threw the boy headlong over its back
and there was a small crack
like the snap of a twig, and the bull
stood over the broken boy
and ran him through with its horns.

Dionysus found the white body lying
in its great red star,
laid anemones on his dead love's open eyes
and a fawn-skin over him to keep
his stopped heart from the cold.
He stood by the boy, watching the red
tendrils branch and twine through the rocks,
and being a god he could not weep
for Ampelos – could neither grieve, nor follow him
down to the land of the dead.

Then Dionysus heard a voice that said,
'Free this love for another, and forget.
When a flower dies, the gardener
must learn to plant again.'

And Dionysus, who never wept,
wept then for Ampelos,
and his tears fell on the boy
and the boy's body started to change.
His feet taking root and the long legs
thickening to stems, his belly twisting
into a stalk that broke into branches
and he shot up his own shape:
leaves grew from his fingers, and up
from the buds of his horns
burst clusters of grapes, hard and green.

Dionysus stood under the vine
that had been Ampelos, and it ripened for him.
He drew some fruit from the stem
like a woman would pull off earrings
and he squeezed them in his fist
till his wrist was laced with red.
Then he licked it, and said: 'You are still alive,
sweet friend, even if you are gone.
You have kept your rosy colour
and you taste of heaven.
I will wear your leaves in my hair instead of snakes
and wind your young shoots round my fennel wand.
I will let you soak through me.'

*And so, wine was made,*
*and we made from it: abandon, delirium,*
*a cure for regret, an end to love and grief.*
*We hold it in our hands: a brief forgetting.*

# THE FISHERMEN'S FAREWELL

Their long stares mark them apart; eyes gone
to sea-colours: grey, foam-flecked

and black in the undertow, blue
as the blue banners of the mackerel, whipping west.

On land, they are smoke-walkers, where each stone
is a standing stone, every circle a stone circle.

They would be rumour if they could, in this frozen
landscape like a stopped sea, from the great stone keels

of Callanish to the walls of Dunnottar and Drum.
They would be less even than rumour:

to be ocean-stealers, to never throw a shadow –
to dream the blank horizon and dread the sight of land.

The drink storms through these men, uncompasses
them, till they're all at sea again.

Their houses, heeled over in the sand:
each ruin now a cairn for kites.

And down by the quay
past empty pots, unmended nets and boats:

this tiny bar, where men sleep upright
in their own element, as seals.

# ARGENTIERA

Under the ruins of the old silver-mine
the sea is wild. Children go in
off these rocks all summer

and the waves, like their lives, raise them up
and let them down,
haul them up and drop them –

except for one swimmer, and the one great wave
that won't stop falling: that takes his legs
and then just holds him under.

## FLAGS AND SALUTES

An exiled king
in the Mediterranean's grim marinas,

vigilant in his polo-neck,
blazer and deck shoes,

the yachting cap trimmed
in gold and stitched

with the crest of his lost principality;
always aware of territorial waters,

never far from a phone
or a glass of gin.

Remembering, every day,
all the hundred rooms

of his palace, the names
of every racehorse in the stable.

Rehearsing again
the homecoming speech in his head.

No flag now but the flag of convenience,
no salute but the barman's empty grin.

# THE FIELD OF FAMINE

*after Ovid*

In the far borders of the ice-lands
lie the barren wastes, home
to glacial Winter,
shivering Pestilence,
and there, in a stony field,
Famine,
dragging at the weeds
with nails and teeth.
Her hair hangs in strings
over a grey face,
sunken eyes, parched
lips and throat. Her skin has dried
hard and thin against her hips
and hollow loins, tight
to the inner organs. Her breasts
are paper bags; the bones
knuckling out of nothing.
Instead of a stomach
there's just an empty hole.

Standing at a safe distance,
the envoy of the goddess
delivered the command,
already feeling the strange
drag of hunger.
She told Famine the name
and the place where she must go.

# WIRE

In this bled landscape
wind moves through the desert bones,
fluting their white notes.

★

Wildfires sweep the hills,
jump the highways. Outside town
fence-posts are burning.

★

The guns go one way,
drugs go the other, over
the desert border.

★

There's crystal meth, coke,
PCP, smack; after that
Tipp-Ex, gasoline.

★

In Juárez tonight
three *decapitados* hang
from the Bridge of Dreams.

★

The mystery lights
are lost souls on the border
crying out for home.

★

*Mesquite and yucca,*
*lechuguilla, creosote*
*bush, Apache plume.*

★

Reading tracks, cutting
for sign and finding nations:
people not our own.

★

The cave's petroglyphs
are Apache: antelope,
deer, their children's hands.

★

The cat rose and fell
on the feeding hummingbird,
tore its wings away.

★

The low moan at night
is the freight train; its sudden
hundred cars of noise.

*

He showed me the place:
*La puerta*, he said. *Door.*
There was nothing there.

*

A million acres
gone, under a flag of smoke,
border to border.

*

*Cholla, prickly pear,*
*the night-blooming cereus,*
*the rare peyote.*

*

The fenced dogs go mad
when they sense their wild cousin:
trickster, coyote.

*

The wilderness blooms
abruptly, into its own
tree of sand and blood.

*

When the road belches,
bellies like a breaching whale,
it's an IED.

*

The coyote walks
through betrayal, grief, horror,
steps through fire and ice.

*

The Apache's long
night-vision sees the runners
cross-haired: the white men.

*

The command comes through
as ghosts scribble the desert:
*You're clear to engage.*

*

*Pronghorn, jack-rabbit,*
*coyote, javelina,*
*skunk, mountain lion.*

\*

*Coyotes* running
people over the border
like sand through the wire.

\*

*Frontera*, she said,
pointing in all directions.
There was nothing there.

\*

On this empty road
there's only Border Patrol
fingering their guns.

\*

Drained water bottles,
the fence in the desert night;
human traces, ghosts.

\*

Rifles and hand-guns
held by twenty-year-old boys
wearing five-point stars.

\*

*Nine points of the law.*
*Good fences make good neighbours.*
Tell that to the dead.

\*

*Western diamond-back,*
*Mojave, prairie, black-tailed;*
*the still copperhead.*

\*

Only the sphinx moth
will find the evening primrose
and her nectary.

\*

The dead jack-rabbit
has dried flat as wood, like a
Texas cricket bat.

\*

I find Our Lady
of Guadalupe out there,
watching through the wire.

\*

Only the eagle
moves in this heat, shimmering
in the blue thermals.

\*

Covering my tracks
I have tied mesquite branches
to the horse's tail.

\*

These are just fences
and the fences are burning.
This is no-man's-land.

\*

See beyond the smoke,
see with the eyes of eagles:
this is no man's land.

# THE HOUSE OF ENVY

*after Ovid*

In a deep ravine, hidden
from the sun and the winds of the air,
sits the House of Envy:
filthy with decay,
wreathed with darkness
and a bitter cold, an endless fog
wound round its running walls.

The goddess struck once at the door
with the end of her spear
and it swung open
revealing Envy
inside, busy at her meal of vipers' meat
which kept her venom fed.
The goddess flinched at the sight.
The creature rose – the skins
and heads of snakes
slipping from her lap –
and limped
slowly towards the door
where she saw her visitor, this
armoured beauty, and shrank
back with a terrible groan
away from the light.
But you could see her plain enough:
bloodless, skew-eyed;
slime dripping from her
hanging mouth.

It's said she would smile
only at the sight of suffering;
the very thought of happiness
kept her from sleep: it eats at her,
wastes her away.
Gnawing at others, gnawing at herself,
she is her own torment.

'Take your staff of thorn and briar,
cloak yourself in cloud
and carry out your task,'
the goddess ordered, starting to chew
the inside of her mouth.
'Trample the flowers, wither the grass,
blight the forests
and bring your taint into the world.
Here is the name. Instil your poison.'
With that, the goddess pushed her spear
hard against the ground,
and in one vault ascended to the upper air.

# FALCONER'S FAREWELL

She kept a cast of merlins
mewed in her own chamber; let him
fletch his shafts with each new
throw of feathers.

He strung his bow with sinew, the very nerve
of a deer, so he'd draw with such speed and gift
he could pin a pair of arrows
on the head of a man, like horns.

When she heard the lark ringing up high
over September, she slipped herself free;
her blue hunger reading the sky – the land
already dropping under her.

His flights missed their mark, slid on the hard,
dry ground, snaked into the grass.
When he looked for them he felt them, snapping
underfoot. And her, nowhere to be found.

## SECOND SIGHT

Last night, the night of the great storm, I was woken late
by someone outside the cottage, in the dark, calling.
Going to the window, my reflection in the glass
was not quite right:
I seemed to stand in a shiver of sea-fire,
clothes sodden, boots brimming with water.
Close up, the glass fogged with my breath.
Trying to wipe it clear I found I couldn't
and I fell back in fright – saw those white eyes, watching,
the skin on the arms slipping off them like sleeves –
and heard the voice of my brother, saying,
'Weep, all you women, for the drowning of me.'

## THE HALVING

(Royal Brompton Hospital, 1986)

General anaesthesia; a median sternotomy
achieved by sternal saw; the ribs
held aghast by retractor; the tubes
and cannulae drawing the blood
to the reservoir, and its bubbler;
the struggling aorta
cross-clamped, the heart
chilled and stopped and left to dry.
The incompetent bicuspid valve excised,
the new one – a carbon-coated disc, housed
expensively in a cage of tantalum –
is broken from its sterile pouch
then heavily implanted into the native heart,
bolstered, seated with sutures.
The aorta freed, the heart re-started.
The blood allowed back
after its time abroad
circulating in the machine.
The rib-spreader relaxed
and the plumbing removed, the breast-bone
lashed with sternal wires, the incision closed.

Four hours I'd been away: out of my body.
Made to die then jerked back to the world.
The distractions of delirium
came and went and then,
as the morphine drained, I was left with a split

chest that ground and grated on itself.
Over the pain, a blackness rose and swelled;
'pump-head' is what some call it
– debris from the bypass machine
migrating to the brain – but it felt
more interesting than that.
Halved and unhelmed,
I have been away, I said to the ceiling,
and now I am not myself.

# THE GHOST OF ACTAEON

'You are sleeping, Mother, and do not know my fate.
I wish you could wake and embrace me, much changed
as I am with the horns and the hair of a stag
and only the eyes and voice the same as Actaeon.
My dogs did what I'd trained them to do: forgive them.
If you see my lost bow, break it: bury it with my bones.
I know you found no sign of them in the woods,
but look again. Look for a freckled coat and not a tunic,
branched antlers not smooth temples, and longer legs
than you remember, that end not in feet, but in hooves.'

# FUGITIVE IN LONDON

I use these streets to disappear;
thirty years of ducking round corners
to throw them off the scent,

losing myself in crowds, diving
underground and coming up
like a cormorant, miles downstream.

Night after night, the same dream
of having murdered someone,
hidden them under the floor.

It got so bad I lifted the boards
to look, to see what I'd done. The boy
I'd killed and buried there was me.

# A & E

It was like wetting the bed
waking up that night, soaked through:
my sutures open again
and the chest wound haemorrhaging.
Pulling on jeans and an overcoat
I called a car to Camberwell, and
in through the shivering rubber doors
presented myself
at that Saturday-night abattoir
of Casualty at King's on Denmark Hill.

At this front-line, behind her desk
and barred window, the triage nurse
was already waving me away –
till I parted the tweed to show her
what I had going on underneath.
Unfashionable, but striking nonetheless:
my chest undone like some rare waistcoat,
with that lace-up front – a black *échelle* –
its red, wet-look leatherette,
those fancy, flapping lapels.

# PLAYGROUNDS

She flashed alive in a fight, as if circling me in some
cold car-park, rolling a knife from hand to hand,
dabbing the air with it. Even her face was drawn
and bladed, as if this was her moment – the one
she'd been waiting for – and she grew thin
and sharp and accurate; all quickness and glint.
Anybody watching might have thought her
a Bacchante or a butcher, but you couldn't be sure.

It was always a blur; the way I remember that time
behind the science block, curled up on the concrete:
the four of them all stood there, around me, kicking,
and me thinking only about the small glass bottle
of milk in my pocket, which my mother had put there
as I left, as I set off for school.

# THE DEAD SOUND

Looking back
I knew it was over:

the way you hear
a pot break

and you can tell,
with no sign

of a crack, just by
the dead sound it makes

that it's gone, that it's
only a matter of time.

# STRINDBERG IN SKOVLYST

## I.

A manor house in ruin. It suits me down to the ground.
A tower to write in,
three rooms for the family, with a kitchen,
and all for fifty crowns a month.
Unbelievably filthy, I have to say: everything
broken, unfinished, abandoned.
In the yard, two floors below, a mongrel
half-heartedly mounts a greyhound; blue flies
are hatching in the dung. It fits my mood.
Wherever you look: neglect, failure,
all the shit you could wish for.
A home away from home.

They laid on quite a show, trying to get us to take the place:
goblets of flaming spirits, the Countess
with a hurdy-gurdy, lying on the floor;
her steward as circus-master, conjurer,
with his not-so-beautiful assistant,
the blonde fat girl in a spangled costume.
All the usual card tricks, which I knew,
but then he got her up to the ceiling on poles, then
whipped them away – and she stayed there,
in the air, levitating above us. And she didn't fall.

I gave them three months' rent after that, up front.

II.

The Countess is mad – today and every day –
quite mad, and this is her menagerie;
the cattle and horses stay outside, eating thatch,
but the rest are residents: cats, poultry, eight huge dogs.
She carries a white lamb, sometimes,
but her favourite is Sky-Leaper, the blind,
ancient cockerel she dandles on her lap.
Like magic, rabbits hop out of coal-scuttles,
turkeys squabble in the bath-tub, eating soap.
With a flourish, she reveals
a litter of white kittens in a drawer
then, shyly, from the front of the sky-blue
off-the-shoulder dress she wears each day,
she pulls a duckling.
A pigeon flies through the window,
followed by the male, who ambles after her,
his lady-love: blowing his crop, dragging
his spread tail through the dirt.
An unearthly screech, then the stately
step of an Indian peacock, rustling down the corridor
towards the room
where two Great Danes
are standing on the shaky bed, coupling.
Speaking of which, here's Hansen,
her steward (and more than *that*, I suspect):
a black-fingered trickster with his
wagging forelock and dice for eyes,
up and about, flaunting
his yellow suit, the peacock feather in his hat.

And behind him, the maid – who I take
for his sister – Martha Magdalene:
sixteen if she's a day, blonde *knullhår*,
barely decent with her predatory mouth
and her dress a size too small.

A three-hander, then, with this shambles for a stage:
this home to pestilence, cluster flies, blowflies, men
and women, Ragnarök, Armageddon –
my crucible will turn this all to gold.
In my head, when the gales are riding wild,
I steer towards catastrophe
then write about it.


III.


*Interior. The upper rooms. Noise of children. Dim summer sunlight through the grimy, curtainless windows. The playwright's wife is boiling sheets, swabbing the floorboards with bleach.*

*Interior. Kitchen. The walls and ceilings black with soot, the tables piled with unwashed dishes, rotting food. A side of mutton hangs from a hook on the wall, just high enough to be out of reach of the dogs. The maid, Martha, is shelling peas.*

*Exterior. The pavilion on the lake. The steward, Hansen, and the playwright in animated conversation, drinking schnapps.*

I confess, with a clink of glasses, to six months' celibacy
at the hand of Artemis, my wife,
but he doesn't understand.

That I hate women but desire them –
hate them *because* I desire them.
The power they have.
That I fear I might go mad.
That I am, already, mad.
He sighs, and tells me his ridiculous stories,
shows me conjuring tricks,
sings the same song over and over again.
I only listen when he shares his hopes
for advancement – the dream of climbing
to the top of the high tree
to rob the nest of its golden egg –
but how the trunk is too smooth to gain purchase,
and the branches too high to catch hold.

*Exterior. Garden. The Countess and the playwright walking between*
*the vegetable plots, overgrown with burdock and nettles, cobbled with*
*turds.*

She was going on about her animals, her *family*,
and I thought of that pack of feral dogs –
vile scavengers – and all the rest:
all the tettered, emaciated beasts.
She said she dreamt she was on top of a high pillar
and all she wanted was to fall.

*Interior. The tower room. Midnight.*

The girl, at my door again. What was I to do
against those lead-grey eyes, the tousled hair,
that young, thick body? That *mouth*?
The bestial ruin stinking in my face.

The snort and rut coming closer.
I ran my thumb down the seam,
opening up the velvet
to touch the hard pod of the bean.
She kissed me like a cat.
Cats kill you at the throat, so I was quickly
over her, and in. Behind the trees
a filament of lightning briefly glowed
and died. Manumission.
And now: the fall.


IV.


The voices in my head are company at last
in these high rooms
in the glove of the night, under a fretted moon.
That gypsy Hansen's out there drunk with a gun
shouting about 'corrupting a minor' and
'raping my sister'. Letting off shots.
I was on her *once*
and all I got out of it was scabies, and now infamy.
I told the Countess that her lover's
just a common thief;
she said, 'My brother, you mean.'

Our bags are packed.
The carriage waits below.
I have stoked the fever enough to spark some fire.
It's dreadful, I tell myself, but there's no other way.
We are above such people.
But now it's done. And now I have my play.

## A VISIT

I was walking through her garden
dead-heading the dried-out stalks,
the faded, stiff remains
of the neighbours' cats,
each one pinned with pine needles
like a punctured Christ.

I passed the tree in flames
hearing the sound of a sword in the air,
the sound of a sword
being drawn from a sheath.
She waits beyond all this
as the glove waits for the hand

till I lower myself onto her, the witch,
burrowing under her clothes
for the breasts: the nipples
nesting in the black, wiry hairs
where I can nose
and suckle.

## BROKEN

He's back in the ghost house
where he, himself, is the ghost.
In this slow silt of neglect
half the lightbulbs are blown, the drawers
jammed full of emptiness; the mail
still drifts unopened by the stair.

Outside the old house,
which his mother would call
broken, a 'broken home',
he's trying to clear his head:
sweeping leaves into piles
that the wind just blows away.

# THE CAVE OF SLEEP

*after Ovid*

Deep inside a hollow mountain there's a cave
where the sun's rays never reach;
the earth around it
breathes out
clouds of fog
into this endless twilight,
this secret dwelling-place
of the god of idle Sleep.
There is no cockerel to summon the dawn,
no geese, no dogs, no beasts of any kind
to break the silence, not even branches
stirring in the breeze. Only stillness here,
and the distant murmur far below
of the River Lethe moving pebbles
as it goes, whispering *sleep, sleep.*
Huge lush poppies stand in rows outside;
herbs steep their juices in the night,
infusing the ground with a slow release,
a mulled gravity.
There are no doors, in case a turning hinge
might creak, and no guardian at the gate.
On a platform in the middle of the cave
is a bed of ebony
thick with dark linens, soft black pillows,
where the god himself
lies, deeply, languidly, at peace.
Around him, on all sides, are empty dreams,

countless as ears of corn
at harvest-time, leaves on the forest trees
or grains of sand along the shore.

The messenger of the goddess enters the chamber,
brushing aside the dreams that stand in her way.
The brightness of her robes begins to fill the cave
and Sleep starts to stir, struggling
to lift his eyelids, heavy in slumber.
Over and over again he tries, then falls back,
head sinking into his chest. At last
he wakes, blinks open his eyes and
hoisting himself up on one elbow,
looks at the woman and smiles.

# DIONYSUS AND THE MAIDEN

*after Nonnus*

I

Her only home was here in this forest, among the high rocks,
sending her long arrows in flight through the standing pines
as if threading nets in the air.
She'd never seen a cup of wine or a perfumed room, or a bed:
she drank chill water from the mountain brook and had only ever
lain with lionesses, newly delivered of their cubs, who licked
her hard white body, whimpering there like dogs.

She was not alone in the woods: the breeze shook her hair, lifted
the edge of her tunic on those bare legs
as she ran on the rocks, climbing
after a huge stag, and stopped; felt for the shaft
and quickly nocked it to the bowstring, drew, and let it loose.

She was not alone: a young shepherd was watching,
trying to call up the breeze to lift her again. He wanted to be
her quiver, her spear, and when he found all her weapons in a cave
he was swept with such longing he kissed her coiled nets
and pressed an arrow to his lips – which is how she found him.

'Save me from this passion, this fire that feeds under my heart!
If you can never love me, as you must know now that I love you,
then to watch your bow-arm tighten and your breast rise and steady
is all I can ever ask, so fix me in the heart to end this hurt . . .'

Despite her shaking fury, her disgust, she drew fast and clean:
pinning the last words back in with his tongue,
filling his mouth with feathers.


II


He was done now with satyrs, took no pleasure in his Bacchae.
Dionysus – he whose colours were never true – had seen her
swimming naked in a pool, seen her again in the flowers:
arms of lily-white, cheeks of the rose, eyes of hyacinth blue.

'If you wish for a chamber in the forest,' he said, 'I will grow
grapevine round a glade strewn with ferns and petals of iris,
and lay a piled bed of dappled fawn-skins there
for you, to rest your head on the shoulder of Dionysus.'

'Touch me or my bow or quiver and you'll follow
that lovesick shepherd . . . Believe me, I will wound
the unwoundable Dionysus. I refuse your bed,
your perfumed hair, your woman's body, even if it's true
your veins beat with the blood of Zeus.
I'll take no man for a lord, and no god either.'
And with that she went plunging into the forest.

For days he tracked her, kept her on high ground
away from the water; let the thirst for it draw her back down.
He opened his arms and darkened the river with wine;
folded his arms, and she drank it down in draughts.
Her world doubled. She turned her eyes round
to the wide yawning lake, and she saw two lakes;

the hills swung around her as her head grew heavy
and her feet slipped under her, under the heavy wing
of sleep, and deep into this: her wedding slumber.

He came to her then, undid the end of the knot, releasing
a teeming fragrance of flowers, and ivy, and vine
with grapes in its leaves as a screen for the bed,
for the stolen bridal, for the pleasure of Dionysus.
He entered her the way light breaks through mountains;
gave her this: his gift of going,
made the noise of a cliff, and fell away.

She woke in her pain to a bed of skins and leaves, her thighs
soaked through. She wept and raged at her abandonment by the gods.
All the gods but one.
She thought to set a sword to her throat, cast herself
rolling off some crag; to cut apart the river where she drank,
burn down the mountains, uproot the forest where she ran.
But it was him she wanted most: to track him and find him and drain
his heart's blood on her dagger's blade. Take his breath away.
She wandered the high hills for weeks, months, into winter,
casting her nets at shadows, pitching her lance at the dark.
With every sound she heard, she freed flocks of arrows into the air,
into the body of the god, she hoped.
But Dionysus *was* air, and she was alone in the woods,
following these tracks
of a beast, or a man, or a god
when they were just her own tracks in the snow.

# THE SHELTER

I should never have stayed here
in this cold shieling
once the storm passed
and the rain had finally eased.

I could make out shapes
inside, the occasional sound:
a muffled crying
which I took for wind in the trees;
a wasp,
stuttering there at the windowsill.
I listened. What looked like
a small red coat
was dripping from its wire hanger.

There was a shift and rustle
coming from the bucket in the corner
by the door; I found, inside,
a crumpled fist of balled-up paper, slowly
uncrinkling.

On the hearth, just legible
in the warm ash, my name and dates,
and above that, in a shard
of mirror left in the frame,
I caught sight of myself, wearing
something like a black brooch at the neck.
Then I looked more closely
and saw what it was.

## PARTYTIME

You were quite the vision last night
I remember, before my vision went.

And I was left,
instead,
with this
falling corridor of edges,
the greased slipway
and its black drop: that
glint of fracture
in the faces, in the disco-ball's
pellets of light,
in the long whiskies I threw back
short and hard.
Streeling I was, and streeling I went
through some heavy gate
I came across –
and left the world on the other side, the dark
slowly calving over me
on the white slope,
on the sledge of night.

You liked my sensitive hands, you said,
but my hands are empty.
I will give you everything
but have nothing to give.

And now: now
I'll fall back

on instinct, compass,
the ghost in the sleeve,
find my way home to a place
so small I can barely stand.
The city has flooded, emptied,
flooded again.
I don't know where I am.
*Your door is near*, someone laughed,
*just around that corner.*
The frightened boy
climbed out of me and ran.

# PUNCHINELLO'S FAREWELL

*after Tiepolo*

Straightening up his sugarloaf hat, he stoops
– all thumbs, fumbling the buttons –
and drops his trousers: staring, blankly,
at these marbled thighs, grey
knees, the mealy, withered shanks.
Lifting the dense lard of his belly, he
spots what he thought he was missing
– his butcher's apostrophe –
and does a little shuffling dance,
half-masted, with a chalky grin.

He'd woken with a spark in his throat
and they'd been at it all morning,
guzzling jug after jug of Valpolicella,
mopping it up with gnocchi.
Made a scene in town with their yells and jokes,
their somersaults and tumbling, crowing
like roosters and gaping at girls:
crowding round them, flicking their skirts,
sniffing below for that soppy smell, that
briny, cowrie-shell tang.

His pal, still holding the neck of a bottle,
is blotto: out cold in the *mezzogiorno* heat.
Hobbling over to a broken bench he squats,
finds the right position and, sheepish,
sniggering, lets out a sludge of wine and macaroni.

He will be gone, soon enough,
when the light turns aubergine,
but a hundred more of him will take his place,
with their conical hats, white suits, thirsts
and hungers, their humpbacks and their beaks.

## THE DREAM HOUSE

For ten years I dreamt of the same house:
until I knew every corridor and cornice, the grain
of the wood in every board, the way light fell
in different rooms at different times of day. Its lines
and angles grew more perfect, dream by dream.

This summer, walking in woods near a town
I'd never been before, I came to this familiar gate
and beyond that saw a path I recognised.
And there it was, with a sign FOR SALE,
among larch and pine and sycamore: the dream house.

I rang the bell, and when the owner came
I asked him if he'd think it very strange
if I showed him round. To the left, I explained,
is the lounge and panelled library; to the right
the long dining-room with the kitchen beyond.
As we went upstairs to the four bedrooms
with their broad bay windows and blue drapes,
I was stopped, dead, on the landing
by a small red door I'd never seen before.
It was new, he said, and just put in that day.

Downstairs, I asked him what he wanted for the house.
He named a price so low I think I showed my surprise,
but said I'd take it. Then he told me why it was cheap:
because it was haunted. But said I shouldn't mind –
it would be fine for me – since I was the ghost.

That was a month ago, and now I have the keys.
I explore, knowing each room like my own body,
until I remember the tiny red door.
The keys are all too big, except for one
the size of a sparrow's claw. I kneel down
and open the lock. And there, in the darkness,
is a miniature house. Through the windows,
in behind the walls, I see my son is safe indoors.
How little he's grown. Look at him!
The boy I dreamt had died ten years before.

# KEYS TO THE DOORS

*for Eilidh*

I loved your age of wonder: your third and fourth
and fifth years spent astonished, widening your eyes
at each new trick of the world – and me standing there,
solemnly explaining how it was done. The moon and stars,
rainbows, photographs, gravity, the birds in the air,
the difference between blood and water.
*In true life?* you would say, looking up
and I would nod, like some broken-hearted sage,
knowing there would be no answers soon
to all the big questions that were left, to cruelty and fear,
to age and grief and death, and no words either.
And you, like me, will sit and shake your head.
*In true life?* Yes, my sweet, strong daughter, I'm afraid
there is all this as well, and this is it: true life.

# CRIMOND

*i.m. Jessie Seymour Irvine*

Daughter of the manse of Dunnottar, then Peterhead
and Crimond, all north-eastern edges over unstill waters,
what softness brought this tune from your young hands?
The tune my father called for every Sunday: the 23rd psalm.
When I hear it now, it's all wet cobbles and the haar
rolling in down the street outside, and him
shaking their hands, sharp in his black and white:
the dog-collar (I knew) cut clean from a bottle of Fairy Liquid.
How far we all are from where we thought we'd be:
those parishioners all vanished long ago; my father – ash
above the crematorium; me, swimming back-crawl
through the valley of the shadow of death, and you –
not even a photograph left of you – the girl who will never
touch again the foot of the cross at Crimond.

# THE HOUSE OF RUMOUR

*after Ovid*

At the world's centre
between earth and sky and sea
is a place where every sound can be heard,
where everything is seen.
Here Rumour lives,
making her home on a mountain-top.
This house stands open
night and day: a dome
of apertures and windows set
like a million eyes at gaze,
steady, unblinking,
no doors or shutters anywhere.
Her walls have ears.
They *are* ears. The whole house
made from thinly-beaten,
resonating bronze, hums
constantly
with words repeating back to themselves
round and round, again
and again: the low susurration
of echoing sound.
No silence anywhere,
just the murmur of voices
like whispering waves
or the last low rolling crush of thunder.
The house is haunted by shadows,
ghosts that come and go, a host of rumours,

the false mixed with the true,
words and phrases, fact, fictions,
fabrications, all confused.
At every turn, a story spreads
and grows and changes, each new teller
adding on to what they've heard.
Here is surveillance, interception;
a multitude of recording angels.
Here lives rash Credulity, reckless Error,
groundless Joy. Whispers
make their home here, alongside
sudden Sedition, tremulous Fear.
Rumour herself
hears everything, sees
everything that happens in the heavens,
in the sea or on the earth;
invigilator, sentinel, echo-chamber,
she misses nothing
misses no one as she sweeps the world.

# THE STRAW MANIKIN

*after Goya*

The hooded penitents have passed – the shackled
*Nazarenos* holding their long candles – and the altar boys,
carrying the trappings of the Passion on their pillows:
the hammer and nails, the crown of thorns, the chalice
and the pliers; the soldiers' flail, the soldiers' dice.

*What shall we give him? The straw man is sick.*
*We'll finish him off, and beat him with sticks.*

The *pasos* have drifted away: statues of full-size
wooden Christs and Virgins painted till they came alive
– glass eyes, glass tears, eyelashes of human hair,
ivory teeth and nails – on floats borne by fifty men,
invisible under curtained palanquins.

*Poor puppet, I think he wants to die.*
*Poor puppet, he wants to die.*

The bands have dispersed. The slow march of the drums
that marked the time, the mournful trumpet
piercing the night. The crowds gone – and the brotherhoods:
*The Star, The Bitterness, Vera-Cruz, The Thirst,*
*The Spearthrow, The Seven Words, Silence.*

*Give him some snail-water, that'll be best,*
*then pitch him, and toss him, until he is dead.*

Four women are left, each holding the corner of a blanket,
laughing at this doll of a man they're flipping up in the air
till he starts to come apart. A fop with rouged cheeks
and a pigtail – a loosened Christ, or Judas, or just a man,
falling: the body spilling chaff, some hanks of straw.

*I think the manikin's ready to die.*
*The manikin's ready to die.*

# THE GOD WHO DISAPPEARS

*after Nonnus*

Born to a life of dying, the boy-god's first death came
when he could barely crawl, the budding horns just there,
nudged among curls, as he played on the floor
with his toys: a knuckle-bone, ball and spinning-top,
golden apples, a tuft of wool, and
on his other side, the thunderbolts of Zeus.

They entered the throne-room's dark,
their round faces smeared with chalk into pale moons,
and they slid forward, drawing their hungry knives.
He saw them in the mirror, looming behind him
in a hundred reflections,
and he watched his body swim through other shapes:
a doubled-up ancient with a face of rain,
a blank-eyed baby, downy youth. Then he saw the mane
of a lion, jaws opening, the sinewed neck
of a bridling horse, the darting tongue
and poison fangs and coils stretching
for the throat of one of the murderers, then
twisting, to the leap of a tiger, the shouldering,
heavy-horned bull, and then suddenly the great bull
shuddered to a stop,
and they started slicing him
to piecemeal; so many blades
he could see in the mirror,
working on the bull-shaped Dionysus.
He followed his image into the glass, and was soon

split and scattered, divided up, diced
into the universe.

\*

He spends his life dying. The god who comes,
the god who disappears. Dismembered,
he is resurrected. He is beside us; beside himself.
Ghost of abandon, and abandoning,
he shatters us to make us whole.

## TILLYDRONE MOTTE

I played my childhood here on this highest edge,
this hill, in this park: my garden
spread out for me two hundred feet below,
the Don coursing through it, out towards the sea.
Fifteen years in every kind of light and weather:
my castle-keep, watchtower,
anchorite's cell, my solitary
proving ground, a vast sounding-board
here amongst the gorse and seabirds.

As the river-terraces below me filled with cloud
I stood over it all, making a ghost, a brocken spectre,
trying to cast the shadow of a man.

I knew all the places to disappear, to go
where you couldn't be seen from the path:
the pillbox, the tree-house, that secret beach
and, hidden above it, the charmed wood. I knew
where the hawthorn tree stands,
bent and fixed like blown smoke,
the sun skimmering in the twist of the river water,
the rough hand of the sea-wind in the elms
and sycamores, the soft courtesy of snow.
I knew where to find the cloaked heron,
the cormorant clergy, where I once saw
the swan in the rapids with the Don in spate,
knew the names of the brothers
that drowned there, at the mill turn
– the Crook of Don – where the river tightens in,

where sweetwater meets the brine reaches. I knew
how it came down through the braes and weirs
to the green sluice under the hill, to coast
its way past Walker's Haugh and Kettock's Mill
to the Devil's Rock, drawing
deep through Tam's Hole and the Pot, over
the Black Neuk of the Brig o' Balgownie
where the river rests before the last pull
through the machair and out
to the sea beyond.

A distant smatter of applause and, seconds later,
I see the flock lifting, down in the valley,
losing itself in the far pines.

What I didn't know was this:
that there would come a time when I would find
the trees unclimbable, the river too fast to ford,
that I would learn it wasn't a motte at all
– this hill where I went to be born –
but a Bronze Age burial cairn,
and not Tillydrone either
– this place where I stood my pale cross –
but *tulach draighionn*, which means,
and has always meant, 'the hill of thorns'.

# FINDING THE KEYS

The set seed and the first bulbs showing.
The silence that brings the deer.

The trees are full of handles and hinges;
you can make out keyholes, latches in the leaves.

Buds tick and crack in the sun, break open
slowly in a spur of green.

\*

The small-change colours of the river bed:
these stones of copper, silver, gold.

The rock-rose in the waste-ground
finding some way to bloom. The long

spill of birdsong. Flowers, all
turned to face the hot sky. Nothing stirs.

\*

That woody clack of antlers.
In yellow and red, the many griefs of autumn.

The dawn light through amber leaves
and the trees are lanterned, blown

the next day to empty stars.
Smoke in the air; the air, turning.

\*

Under a sky of stone and pink
faring in from the north and promising snow:

the blackbird.
In his beak, a victory of worms.

The winged seed of the maple,
the lost keys under the ash.

## ON THE ISLAND

We were displaced birds, and weathered here
a winter: long wing under heavy wing,
grey wing over brown.
The sun slipped into the sea and sank,
and our clambering hearts fell in
with the draw and plunge
of the wave in the bay, the surf

breaking, drowning itself
deep in the sand.
The moments of shaking
shudder through me still.
Our mouths are stopped; my body
rests against yours now, my hand
sleeps in your hand.

# GLASS OF WATER AND COFFEE POT

*after Chardin*

These rooms of wood, of tongue-and-groove, open out
on a garden of white-washed walls and a maple tree,
a new Spring bright among the weathered stone and brick.
We find things that are old and used, well-made, well worn
and beautiful because of this. The balance
intimate between that glass of water's clarity and light
and the pot's grave darkness: an order so luminous
and fine you needn't measure it with a rule, just look.
The papery whiteness of the garlic heads is the same light
held in the water glass, the same light lifting a gleam
from the blackened coffee pot that's somehow managed
to make it through, to find harmony here
on this stone shelf, happiness of the hand and heart,
to keep its heat and still pour clean and true.

## PORT NA H-ABHAINNE

We walked the cliff of Portnahaven
listening to the grey seals sing
on Orsay and Eilean Mhic Coinnich
across the little harbour.

Were they singing for the love
of being here in this place, like us,
far from griefs – and were they also
singing, as we were, to each other?

## THE KEY

The door
to the walled garden, the place
I'd never been,
was opened

with a simple turn
of the key
I'd carried with me
all these years.

# Notes & Acknowledgements

**Annunciation**

The fresco 'The Annunciation' by Fra Angelico in Museo Nazionale di San Marco in Florence.

**The Coming God**

from *Dionysiaca*, Books IX, XIV.

**1964**

The year of the typhoid epidemic in Aberdeen.

**Under Beinn Ruadhainn**

Beinn Ruadhainn: (Gaelic) 'summit of the red place'; 'Ruadhainn' anglicised as 'Ruthven', pronounced *Riven*

horn-daft: quite mad

havering: babbling, speaking nonsense

glaikit: vacant, idiotic

gilping: spurting, spilling

foosty: mouldy, gone bad

**Corryvreckan**

The third biggest whirlpool in the world; to be found between Jura and Scarba.

**Dionysus in Love**

from *Dionysiaca*, Books X, XI, XII.

**The Field of Famine**

from *Metamorphoses*, Book VIII.

**Wire**

*coyotes*: popular name for those who smuggle Mexicans over the
US border.

**The House of Envy**

from *Metamorphoses*, Book II.

**Falconer's Farewell**

mewed: put a hawk in a quiet place to moult.

**Strindberg in Skovlyst**

In the summer of 1888, Strindberg rented rooms with his wife,
Siri von Essen, and their children, in the manor house at Skovlyst,
near Copenhagen. The marriage had collapsed but the family was
still travelling together around Europe. In exile, Strindberg had
recently fallen heavily under the influence of the writings of Nietzsche.
During the summer in Skovlyst, he wrote – amongst other things –
his most famous play, *Miss Julie*.

The poem incorporates images from *Miss Julie* and some adapted
original lines: two from the play and one from a contemporary letter
from Strindberg to Verner von Heidenstam.

*knullhår*: (Swedish) pronounced *knool-hoer*: a neologism, literally
'fuck-hair', suggestive of dishevelled, post-coital tangles.

**The Cave of Sleep**

from *Metamorphoses*, Book XI.

**Dionysus and the Maiden**

from *Dionysiaca*, Books XV, XVI.

**Punchinello's Farewell**

The drawing by Giovanni Battista Tiepolo notionally titled '*Due
Pulcinella, uno disteso e l'altro seduto*' ('Two Punchinellos, one stretched
out and the other seated') in the Fondazione Giorgio Cini, San Giorgio
Maggiore, Venice.

### Crimond

Jessie Seymour Irvine (1836–87) was the daughter of Alexander Irvine, a Church of Scotland minister. She wrote the tune 'Crimond' in her teens, and it is now the standard setting for the 23rd psalm.

### The House of Rumour

from *Metamorphoses*, Book XII.

### The Straw Manikin

The painting 'El Pelele' ('The Straw Manikin') by Francisco de Goya, in the Prado, Madrid. The poem describes the processions of Semana Santa (Holy Week) which, in some parts of Spain, culminate in the tossing and dismembering of a straw doll. The four couplets in italic are rough translations of parts of 'El Canto del Pelele', a Spanish children's song.

### The God Who Disappears

from *Dionysiaca*, Book VI.

### Tillydrone Motte

The setting is Seaton Park, Old Aberdeen.

brocken spectre: (German: *Brockengespenst*), also called 'brocken bow' or 'mountain spectre', the magnified shadow thrown by a climber standing on high ground looking down into mist or cloud with the sun behind. The head of this apparently huge figure is usually encircled by a halo of coloured, diffracted light, called a 'glory'.

*tulach draighionn*: (Gaelic) pronounced *tooluch dryun*.

### Glass of Water and Coffee Pot

The painting by Jean-Baptiste-Siméon Chardin, in the Carnegie Museum of Art, Pittsburgh.

### Port na h-Abhainne

Port na h-Abhainne: (Gaelic) 'harbour at the river'; a village in the south-west of Islay, anglicised as Portnahaven, pronounced *Port na haa-vin*.

Acknowledgements are due to the editors of the following:

*Agenda, American Scholar, Atlantic, Brick, Granta, Guardian, London Review of Books, New Republic, New York Review of Books, New Yorker, Poem, Poetry, Poetry London, Poetry Review, Threepenny Review.*

'Partytime' was commissioned by Nick Barley for the Edinburgh Book Festival website and subsequently published in *Elsewhere* (Cargo/McSweeney's). Carol Ann Duffy commissioned 'Annunciation' for the *Guardian* and 'The Halving' for *Jubilee Lines* (Faber). 'Tillydrone Motte' was commissioned by Gareth Evans for *Towards Re-Enchantment: Place and Its Meanings* (Artevents).

My thanks to Marina Warner for sending me back to the *Dionysiaca,* and to Don Paterson – as always – for sending me back...

I am most grateful to the Lannan Foundation for allowing me a month in Marfa, Texas, at the time of the Rockhouse Fire.